RUTH
A Love Story

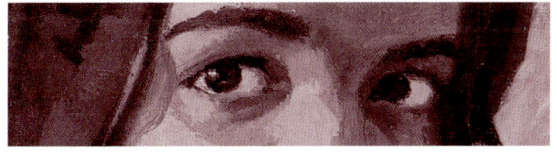

Owen A. Dorn

NORTHWESTERN PUBLISHING HOUSE
Milwaukee, Wisconsin

Dedicated to the God-fearing women who have had an impact on my life

Cover illustration: Johnson and Fancher
Interior illustrations: Troy Allen, Samantha Burton, Frank Ordaz

Northwestern Publishing House
1250 N. 113th St., Milwaukee, WI 53226-3284
www.nph.net
© 2003 Northwestern Publishing House
Published 2003
Printed in the United States of America
ISBN 0-8100-1348-7

CONTENTS

They have been referred to as the saints, the Hebrews, the Israelites, a remnant, and the church. They are God's people—his *chosen* people. They belong to him; so precious that he would go to impossible lengths to overcome the gulf that separates them from himself. You and I are among them.

The books in this series are a recital of the life and times of some of them—Noah, Jacob, Ruth, David, Jonah, Paul, and others. Their stories involve conflict and resolution, pain and tragedy, despondency and renewal. They present disturbing images from the underbelly of human depravity, and visions of untold glory that transport us to the soaring heights of ultimate conquest. The plots and settings are drawn from the living record of the Bible. Series authors and editors were careful to remain faithful to that record. Yet today's sophisticated reading audiences demand background and description. They relate to narrative. In an effort to make the text come alive, each story in this series is presented in a natural framework designed for this audience.

In these stories we see God's people wrestling with their humanity and struggling to find respite for their souls. Each story is unique in its own right. Yet two common threads run through the fabric of their stories and ours. The first is the thread of the bitter curse of sin. The second is the golden thread of salvation in Christ Jesus. We can readily identify with both, for we share these same two themes with all of God's people. Their stories, like ours, rest forever in God's abiding grace.

Kenneth Kremer, Series Editor

In the long history of the Old Testament, God's people frequently lost their focus. Time after time the promised Messiah of God's covenant had been forgotten or ignored by his people, Israel.

But God never forgot. And with the divine wisdom that humans can never hope to fathom, he often kept his promise of a Savior alive through unlikely people such as the woman featured in this book.

This is the story of Ruth. In it we see Ruth, a Moabitess, and her Jewish mother-in-law, Naomi, facing famine, poverty, starvation, and alienation. Their story spans the full spectrum of human emotions. We get a glimpse of the Lord's guiding hand, actively shaping their lives, bending their will to his own.

It is also a story of intrigue, of women surviving in a culture dominated by men, of Jewish tradition and law, of unflinching loyalties, and of enduring compassion. The setting is common, as are its three principal characters. But the unfolding events of this remarkable narrative are anything but common. Nor is its underlying message of redemption and grace.

Above all, the story of Ruth is a love story—of God's love for Ruth, Naomi, and Boaz; of Ruth's love for God, which overflowed in her cherished relationship with Naomi; and finally, of the mutual love between Ruth and Boaz—a mature and understanding love that moved God's history one step closer to fulfillment in the promised Messiah.

This is the story of Ruth, a foreign woman of gentile ancestry, whom God chose not only to live as an Israelite through faith but also to serve all of mankind as a critical

A LOVE STORY

link in the genealogical line of God's coming Christ. In the absence of her story, the story of our redemption would not have been complete.

Naomi shivered even though the breeze was hot and dry. Pulling her black cloak around her shattered life, she cast one last look at her son's fresh grave. Then she turned, lifted her shoulders, and slowly walked away.

Drought had driven her family out of their homeland. Naomi, Elimelech, and their two sons had lived in the hill country of Judah, west of the Dead Sea, near the village of Bethlehem. Usually this was a rich land—a land capable of producing a substantial harvest of wheat and barley—a land eagerly nourishing grapevines, olive groves, and fig trees. But the last ten years or so had been unusual: the rains had failed, the crops had withered, and famine had followed. With the drought had come much suffering and hardship for the people of Judah, who made their living from the land.

But the rains had not stopped falling in the high plateau across the Dead Sea called Moab. In Moab there was hope. In Moab the bountiful fields of grain beckoned. Naomi's husband, Elimelech, had chosen Moab as a refuge from the famine for his family. He did so even though bitterness and hatred divided the Hebrew Judaites and the pagan inhabitants of Moab. Elimelech seemed to have no other choice. He had to do something. No longer able to support his wife and their two sons, Mahlon and Kilion, in Judah, Elimelech had done a reasonable thing by moving his family to this life-sustaining land that was Moab. It was to be a temporary move. Moab could never become their homeland. As soon as the rains again fell in Judah, Elimelech had every intention of returning his family to Bethlehem in Judah, the place of his ancestral home. Certainly the rains would come soon enough. After all, *Bethlehem* means "House of Bread."

But Elimelech's plans were not God's plans. More than ten years after moving to Moab, Naomi was still living there, in Moab—alone.

Well, almost alone.

Elimelech had been the first to succumb to the grave—leaving his widow and sons to cope on their own in a foreign land and a foreign culture. And now, after ten years in Moab, Naomi's sons were also gone. Naomi had just buried her second son—the last member of her family. Now the question was, who would provide for her?

Oh, Naomi's sons had married, but her Moabite daughters-in-law, Orpah and Ruth, were now widows themselves. They certainly could not take care of aging Naomi. Besides, this land was not her home, nor was it the land of her God. Chemosh was the national god of Moab—a god who demanded the sacrifice of children! So when word reached Moab that the Lord had finally blessed Judah with rain—that people could again raise figs and olives, wheat and barley in Bethlehem—Naomi prepared to go home.

But Naomi's plans to return to her homeland—the land that had long ago been given to Abraham, Isaac, and Jacob, the land of God's promise—raised new questions about the future plans of Orpah and Ruth. They would certainly stay here in Moab. Even though they were now widows, their families would provide for them. But Naomi had come to love them. Leaving them behind would not be easy.

Judah and Moab

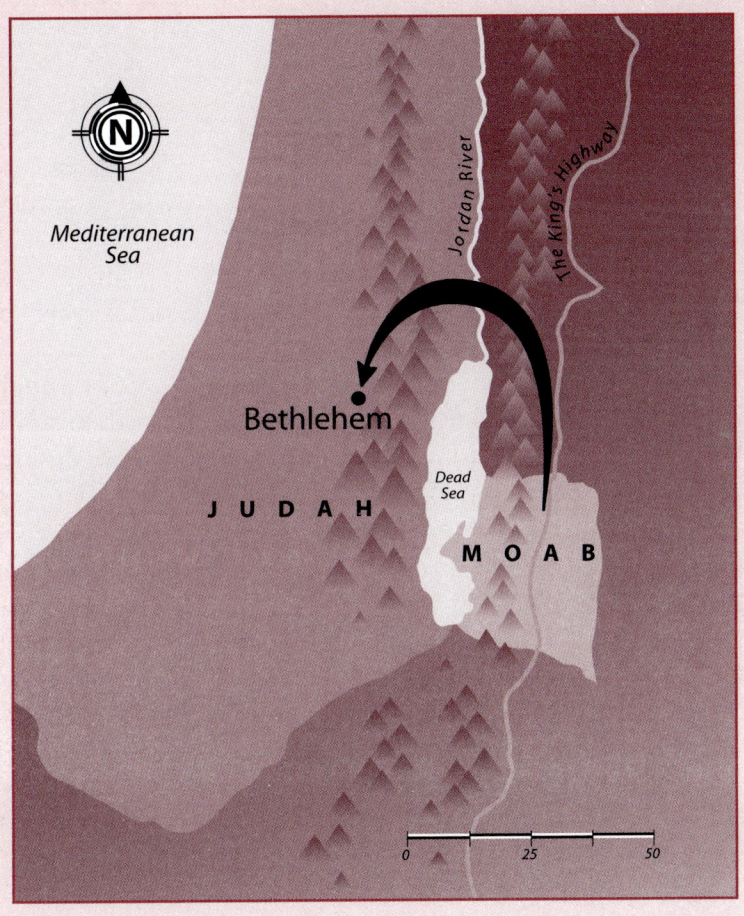

Mediterranean
Sea

Jordan River

The King's Highway

Bethlehem

J U D A H

Dead
Sea

M O A B

0   25   50

A JOURNEY HOME

Naomi had made up her mind at her son's grave. She got up with the sun, and with mixed emotions she packed her meager belongings into her satchel, walked out the door, and began the difficult, 50-mile trek to Bethlehem. As was customary, her daughters-in-law fell in beside her, ready to accompany her for the first part of her long journey home.

Naomi appreciated their thoughtfulness. She found it comforting to begin the lonely trip with loved ones by her side, supporting her and keeping her company. As the three women walked, they talked about little things—the warble of a familiar bird, the shadow of a cloud on a ripening wheat field, the wriggly path of a snake on the dusty road.

Finally, they came upon a lone tree that hugged the road. Naomi stopped to rest in its shadow. She realized the time had come to steel herself for going on alone—Orpah and Ruth had traveled far enough. She turned to them: "It's time for the two of you to go back to your mothers' homes. You've been exceptionally kind to my sons and to me, and I pray that the Lord will be as kind to you as you were to us. May he grant you a home with another husband."

Then she kissed them good-bye.

But they did not move—they would not leave the mother-in-law they had come to love. Instead, they tearfully insisted, "We want to go back with you to your people."

Naomi knew that wouldn't work. For one thing, she had no income; she would not be able to support them when they got to Bethlehem. She also knew that marriage was just about the only option available to women in Judah. Certainly her womb could no longer provide sons for them to marry. And there was little chance that foreigners—hated Moabites at that—would find husbands among the men of Bethlehem. "No, my daughters," she said. "You must go back home to Moab. I am too old to provide husbands for you by having more sons. And even if an old woman like me could have children, would you stay single and wait for them to grow up? No, my daughters, go home."

Perplexed, Orpah and Ruth began to cry again. Orpah was torn. But she finally yielded to Naomi's logic. Although she dearly loved her mother-in-law, living as a stranger in Judah seemed impossible. Knowing she would never see Naomi again, Orpah gave her one last kiss good-bye, turned, and began the lonely walk back to her family—and her gods.

Ruth, however, would not be deterred. She clasped her mother-in-law's hands between her own and would not leave. Naomi tried once more: "Look, Ruth, your sister-in-law has gone back to her family and to her gods. Go back with her."

But Ruth tightened her grip and pleaded: "Please don't make me leave you. I'll go wherever you go, and I'll stay wherever you stay. Your people will be my people, and your God will be my God. Wherever you die, I will die, and I will be buried there with you."

Staying in Moab was no longer an option for Ruth. She was no longer a Moabite at heart, nor a worshiper of Chemosh. Naomi was the only person that she knew who worshiped the true God. She would cling persistently to her and, for the rest of her life, live among those who loved God.

A JOURNEY HOME

Naomi could no longer argue against Ruth's unswerving faith. Her loyalty and determination seemed to overwhelm reason and logic. Naomi saw that she had little choice but to give in. And so the two women continued toward Bethlehem together.

The two women continued to follow the King's Highway through the rolling plains of Moab until they were north of the Dead Sea. Then they trudged west toward the Jordan River. When they neared Jericho, the weary women forded the Jordan, carrying their sandals and cooling their hot, tired feet in the shallow river. After another night of restless sleep under a brilliant blanket of stars, they arose early and continued westward through the hot, desolate wilderness of Judah.

Naomi and Ruth had been pushing themselves for five grueling days when they finally entered the grassy hills of central Judah. Soon the village of Bethlehem lay before them, with its modest whitewashed houses huddled on the hillside and ripening fields of grain stretched out below.

Naomi and Ruth had arrived in Bethlehem just as the barley harvest was beginning. They followed the footpaths between the grain fields where the men were rhythmically swinging their bronze sickles. For the first time in many years, the harvest of golden grain was more than adequate for the people who lived here. Then the path gently rose up from the fields, leading the two weary travelers into the village marketplace.

The women of the village paused from their daily chores and openly scrutinized them. Who were these two women?

Ruth was a stranger and Naomi was not the same woman she had been when she had left Bethlehem. Her face was lined, her temples prematurely gray, and she walked with a defeated, lethargic gait. Ten years and life's tragedies had taken their toll.

Some wondered out loud, "Can this be Naomi?" Hearing the women's question, Naomi turned to them and said: "Don't call me Naomi. Rather, call me Mara, because the Almighty has made my life bitter, not sweet. When I went away my life was full, but now my life is empty."

God had uprooted Naomi and then taken her family. Now he had brought her back to Bethlehem in poverty. Despair ate at her soul. Yes, there was faithful Ruth, but Ruth was not her own flesh and blood.

The Moabites

When their combined flocks and herds glutted the land they shared, Abraham and his nephew Lot parted company. Lot eventually settled in Sodom, which was quite possibly located at the southern end of the Dead Sea. A few years later, God's justice destroyed wicked and unrepentant Sodom. His compassion, however, spared Lot and his two daughters.

After their escape from God's holy wrath, Lot's daughters plotted to preserve the family lineage. They got their father drunk and slept with him—each conceiving a son. One son, named Ben-Ammi, became the ancestor of the Ammonites. The other son was Moab, ancestor of the Moabites.

Hundreds of years later, the descendants of Lot (Moabites) and the descendants of Abraham (Israelites) met again. In a time of famine, the Israelites had followed Joseph, Abraham's great-grandson, to Egypt. There in Egypt the people of Israel lived in servitude for generations.

Then, following the miracles we know of as the ten plagues and the Passover event, the Israelites followed Moses back to their God-promised homeland of Canaan. The last segment of their 40-year journey led them north on the King's Highway along the east coast of the Dead Sea—to the territory then inhabited by the Moabites. In this encounter the descendants of Moab refused to let the Israelites pass through their territory, forcing them to swing eastward and circle around Moab to reach the Land of Promise.

This Moabite rebuff did not deter the Israelite men from getting involved with the women of Moab. Before the Israelites entered Canaan, attractive Moabite women seduced many of the Israelite warriors. Some of God's people were even drawn into the pagan idol worship of these people, sacrificing to Chemosh, the god of Moab— a god that the Bible calls detestable.

Angered, the God of Israel sent down a plague, killing thousands of Israelites.

At the time of Ruth, Jewish people still spoke of Moabite women with disdain and disgust.

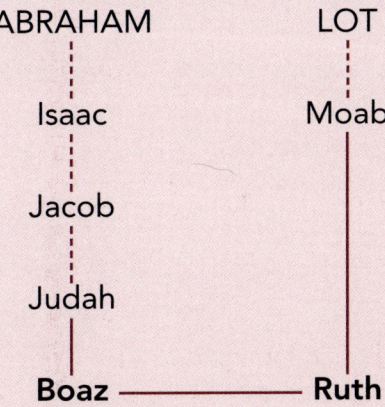

ABRAHAM   LOT

Isaac   Moab

Jacob

Judah

Boaz ——————— **Ruth**

Gleaning

As reapers moved through the fields, grasping handfuls of grain and cutting the stalks with sickles, some stalks would fall to the ground. Stalks that dropped were allowed to remain where they fell. The gleaners—orphans, widows, and the homeless—followed the reapers. They were permitted to gather the random stalks. This meager portion of grain was possibly all that stood between them and starvation. In addition, the grain at the edges of the field, which was difficult to cut, was left unharvested. The poor were welcome to gather that portion into the folds of their long veils as well.

It is quite likely that Jesus' disciples were merely carrying on the commonly recognized tradition of gleaning when some Pharisees challenged them for laboring on a holy day (Matthew 12:1,2).

Ruth and Naomi found a modest place to stay. They would make it into a home—at least they had a roof over their heads. But they wondered how they would support themselves. How would they keep from starving to death? As Ruth pondered that question, she remembered seeing women gathering grain behind the harvesters in the fields outside of town. A distant memory seeped into her thoughts. Naomi had once told her about a provision in the Law of Moses—a provision that might offer some hope. It pertained to widows and foreigners. It stated that as reapers harvested their grain, they were obligated to leave some of the grain uncut. And they were forbidden from going back to harvest the grain they had missed or dropped. Poor widows and foreigners could walk in those same fields and gather whatever leftover grain they could find.

Ruth knew that she and Naomi could take advantage of this charitable law. It was their legal right. Both were widows, and Ruth was a foreigner. But there was something else to be considered here: Naomi had once been the mistress of Elimelech's substantial household. Elimelech's ancestral land holdings were still intact, of course, lacking a male heir to lay claim to the property.

Ruth knew her beloved mother-in-law would find it distressing to publicize her poverty by gleaning among the poor. Ruth didn't want Naomi to be embarrassed in front of her friends and relatives in Bethlehem. So she pleaded with Naomi: "Please let me go and work in the fields. I'll gather grain in the fields of anyone who'll be kind enough to let me."

MEETING, NOT BY CHANCE

Relieved by her daughter-in-law's gracious offer, Naomi gratefully gave her permission. "Go ahead, my daughter."

Early the next morning, Ruth lifted her cape from the hook near the door and quietly slipped out. Encouraged by the promising bright sunrise, she headed toward the fields. Before long, she could hear the faint thwack of sickles shearing stalks of barley. As the sound grew stronger, she could see the reapers grasping handfuls of grain and cutting the stalks. Other workers followed, binding the stalks into sheaves.

When Ruth reached the workers, she saw one of the men issuing orders. He seemed to be in charge. She approached him with her head bowed and asked, "Please allow me to glean behind your men and also to gather some of the grain standing in the field." Receiving permission, Ruth fell in behind the harvesters and began to pick up the grain that had been carelessly left behind. She was determined to gather enough food to sustain herself and her beloved mother-in-law.

This field belonged to a man named Boaz. Though Ruth did not know this, Boaz was a close relative of Elimelech, Ruth's deceased father-in-law. Ruth had not come to this particular field by chance—God had set his plan in motion.

Ruth paced herself. She worked hard and long under the burning sun before she finally sat down to rest in the shade of the crude shelter set up for the field workers. Just then, Boaz arrived in the field. He had come from the village to see how his harvesters were doing. He greeted them, "The Lord be with you!" and they responded, "The Lord bless you!" Then he caught sight of Ruth, sitting in the shelter. "Who is that young woman?" he asked his foreman.

The foreman answered, "She's the young Moabite who came back with Naomi. Early this morning she came out in the field and politely asked me if she could gather grain behind the reapers. I said she could, and she's been on her feet working steadily ever since. She just now sat down in the shelter to rest."

Boaz looked at Ruth once more. He hesitated, then walked over to her. "Listen, my daughter, please feel free to keep gleaning in my fields. Follow my reapers, but stay back and glean near the servant girls who are working behind them. Whenever you get thirsty, go and get a drink from the water jars sitting in the shade of the shelter. And don't worry about being harassed while you work in my fields; I've ordered my young men to keep their hands off you."

Overwhelmed by his kind offer, Ruth bowed down to the ground in a gesture meant to honor the master of the field. "Why are you being so helpful to me—a foreigner?" she asked.

With compassion in his eyes, Boaz looked down at Ruth and said, "I know about the tragedies that befell you and your mother-in-law, Naomi, in Moab. And I've heard what you've done for your mother-in-law since your husband died—how you left your parents and your homeland and came here to live with people who are strangers. May the Lord God of Israel, under whose wings you have come to take refuge, richly reward you for what you've done!"

"I'm not even one of your servants, and yet you have comforted and reassured me," Ruth replied. "I can't thank you enough for your kindness."

Then, with a grateful heart, Ruth went back into the field and continued to glean. When lunchtime came, Boaz was still out in the field with his workers. When the harvesters gathered near the shelter to eat, Boaz again singled out Ruth. "Come, eat," he urged as he gestured toward the food that had been set out. "Please have some of this bread and dip it in the vinegar sauce."

Hunger gnawing at her empty stomach, Ruth nodded and took a piece of bread. It was a welcome treat, and the sour vinegar sauce refreshed her mouth, dry and pasty from hours of physical labor.

The kindness of Boaz didn't stop there. He even offered Ruth some of the fresh grain his workers had roasted in a pan over an open fire. She again accepted his offer, ate until she was full, and still had some grain left to take home to Naomi.

When Ruth finally went back to work, Boaz gave his servants an order: "Let her gather grain—even from the bundles. As a matter of fact, pull some grain out of the bundles and leave it for her to gather. And don't give her a hard time about it."

Ruth continued to gather grain the rest of the day. As the evening shadows began to blanket the grain fields, her aching back could take no more. Slowly, she stood up and carried the load she had gathered to the threshing floor—a leveled area of hard-packed earth. She pounded handfuls of the barley stalks on the hard surface, freeing the kernels of grain. Then she gathered up the barley in her cape—enough to fill half a bushel basket. With that much she could make 20 loaves of bread for Naomi and herself.

Bone-weary, but thankful to her God for such unexpected blessings, Ruth hurried home to share the fresh kernels and the news of the day with Naomi. And, of course, she would give her beloved mother-in-law the roasted grain she had not been able to finish at lunch.

Naomi was astonished when she saw all the grain. She couldn't believe her eyes, and the questions she had regarding Ruth's good fortune poured out of her mouth: "Where did you glean? Where did you work? Who was the man who treated you with so much kindness?"

"I worked in a field owned by a man named Boaz," Ruth replied. Then she began to tell Naomi all that Boaz had said and done for her.

"May the Lord bless him" said Naomi, "even as he continues to show his loving kindness to both the living and the dead." Then Naomi told Ruth that Boaz was a close relative. She explained that this was one of those kindred relationships in which one person becomes responsible for taking care of others.

Could it be possible that Boaz would continue to provide for his poverty-stricken relatives? Might this relative solve their financial problems? The ancient law made it clear that a kindred relative was obligated to see that the property remained in the family. If Naomi had to sell her husband's property after harvest was over, might Boaz possibly buy it?

Ruth continued to tell Naomi about her day. "He even

told me to come back and continue gleaning behind his workers until they finish harvesting all his grain."

"That's wonderful, my daughter. And it's a good idea to glean near the young women who work in his fields. Even though you are a Moabite, I'm sure you'll be safe with them. If you went to glean in someone else's field, it's very possible that someone might assault you."

So Ruth continued to enjoy the favor and protection of Boaz—gathering grain in his fields. And Naomi continued to ponder the possibilities.

Harvesting and Threshing

In Judah, grain was harvested during a seven-week period lasting from mid-April to mid-June. Reapers cut the grain stalks with wooden sickles that had sharpened pieces of flint embedded in them to form a blade. Barley stalks were cut near the top, so that more of the plant would be left for sheep to graze on after harvest. Binders followed the reapers, tying the stalks of grain into bundles called *sheaves*.

Workers then loaded the sheaves onto donkeys or into carts and took them to a patch of hardened clay called the *threshing floor*. There workers separated the grain from the straw stems by beating the grain with sticks or using oxen to trample it. Sometimes they used a threshing board or sled. This was a simple wooden board with stones or iron spikes fixed underneath. Oxen dragged the sled—weighted by the driver and perhaps a child—to loosen the kernels of grain and break up the stalks.

After threshing, harvesters separated the grain from the chaff, which consisted of bits of straw and the outer husk. This was the process of *winnowing*. Workers tossed the grain into the air with a five-pronged winnowing fork so that the breeze could blow the chaff away. The grain was heavier than the chaff and fell to the ground. Any bits of waste or weeds that remained in the grain was then sifted out by shaking the grain in a large sieve. The grain was then stored in earthenware jars or in a dry pit or cistern located in a separate room of the house.

A good harvest was a joyous time. This was usually a time to celebrate. Each evening during threshing time a feast was prepared.

As Naomi considered the possibilities, another idea began taking shape in her fertile imagination. It might only have been a remote possibility, but the fact remained that Boaz had singled out Ruth as the special recipient of his generosity and kindness. He obviously cared about Ruth. He had urged her to spend the entire harvest season gleaning grain in his fields. Was it possible that in his kindness he would continue to provide for Ruth, and her mother-in-law, in a more *permanent* arrangement? Would he, close relative that he was, consider a marriage with Ruth? If such a union were possible, it wasn't so far-fetched to imagine Ruth and Boaz bearing a son. In such a scenario, the child of Boaz and Ruth would be the legal heir of the property that Elimelech and his sons had left behind.

One evening, after Ruth had come home from another taxing day in the field, Naomi cautiously approached her with a proposition. "Ruth, I've been thinking about your future—wondering how you'll be provided for after the harvest is over. And I've come to the conclusion that I should try to find you a good home. I'm quite sure that Boaz—whom you will remember is a close relative of my husband—will be in charge of the threshing floor tonight. After he and his men have finished sifting the chaff from the day's grain, his men will head home for the night. But Boaz will stay out at the threshing floor to guard the grain."

Ruth looked at her without blinking. Where was this going?

SEEING THE POSSIBILITIES

Naomi continued, "Here is what I have in mind. I'd like you to freshen up, put on a little perfume and your best clothes, and go down to the threshing floor. If you get there a little early, be sure to keep out of sight until Boaz has finished his evening meal and settles in for the night. Then, when he has fallen asleep, I want you to do something that will show him that you want him to marry you. Quietly approach him, lift up the robe that covers his feet, and lie down there. The rest is up to him. He will tell you what to do next."

Ruth understood the risk she would be taking if she did what Naomi was asking. Boaz could consider her actions brazen and forward. He could reject her as a loose woman. But Ruth also did not think that was what would happen. She was confident that Boaz had come to know her as a woman of integrity and high moral character.

On the other hand, Boaz could take advantage of her. They would be alone in the dark of night, and she was a lowly woman from Moab. He could choose to have his way with her with no thought of marriage. But, again, that outcome seemed unlikely. Everything Ruth had seen and heard of Boaz shouted to her that he was a man of flawless character. He had always treated her with kindness and respect. She trusted him and had come to care for him. And she was confident that he cared for her as well. No, Boaz could be trusted. He would never mistreat her in that way. Ruth would follow Naomi's plan; she would go to him.

So Ruth told Naomi, "I will do whatever you think is best."

Ruth bathed, dabbed perfume on her body, and slipped into her best garment. When she was ready, she threw her cape over her shoulders, stepped outside, and headed for the threshing floor. When she got there, she stayed in the shadows, watching as Boaz ate and drank to his heart's content.

Finally, Boaz stood up and ambled drowsily to the far end of the grain pile, looking for a comfortable place to sleep. Finding a spot that looked promising, he lay down, covered himself with his cloak, and, using the grain as a pillow, settled in for the night.

Ruth waited. When she was sure he was sleeping soundly, she quietly walked over to him, uncovered his feet, and lay down.

In the middle of the night, Boaz awoke with a start. Wondering what had awakened him, he rolled over to find a more comfortable position. As he turned, he realized that a woman was lying at his feet.

"Who are you?" he asked in the darkness.

"It's me, your servant Ruth. I know you are a close relative who can take care of me, so please spread the corner of your garment over me."

Boaz immediately understood her request—Ruth was asking him to marry her. He answered: "May the Lord bless you, my daughter. By choosing me instead of one of the younger men, you have shown even greater kindness than when you left your home and family to serve God and your mother-in-law, Naomi. Everyone in Bethlehem knows you are a respectable woman, so don't be afraid. I will do what you ask."

SEEING THE POSSIBILITIES

This was a marriage in the eyes of God. Ruth and Boaz had each freely agreed to become husband and wife.

A plan began to form in Boaz' mind. Not only would he marry Ruth, but he would also take care of Naomi by buying her deceased husband's property and keeping it in Elimelech's family. There was, however, an obstacle that first had to be overcome. Boaz knew that a closer relative had first rights to making an offer to purchase the property. He explained the situation to Ruth. "There is a man who is more closely related to Elimelech than me. He has a legal right to buy the property of Naomi's family. Stay here by me the rest of the night. In the morning I will discuss the matter with the man to see if he wants to carry out this responsibility. If not, as surely as the Lord lives, I will purchase the land."

Boaz was a shrewd businessman. He speculated that the relative who held the first legal right to purchase the land would be interested in buying Naomi's property, but would not be interested in marrying Ruth. Yes, that would be part of his strategy when he negotiated with the man in the morning.

While Boaz planned, Ruth lay back down and fell asleep once again—trusting her future to the kindness and wisdom of Boaz. Above all this, Ruth believed that God was in control of all things and that he would find a way to bring his love to bear in this and every circumstance of her life.

Boaz too fell asleep. But before dawn, he awoke. His waking thoughts were for Ruth's welfare. He knew that even though he and Ruth were now married in God's sight, Ruth's reputation would be ruined if anyone knew she had spent the night with him on the threshing floor. Furthermore, his engagement to Ruth must remain a secret until the matter of Naomi's property was legally resolved. So when Ruth woke up, Boaz quickly poured six scoops of barley into the folds of her cape and sent her back to Naomi before it was light enough for anyone to recognize her. Then he headed back into town to carry out his plan.

Ruth quietly slipped into Bethlehem in the gray of pre-dawn. She entered her house quietly, but Naomi was awake. "How did it go, my daughter?" Naomi asked, trying to restrain her eagerness. Had her hopes been realized? Or had they been dashed?

Ruth understood that the events of that night would transform her life. And she knew that the outcome of the negotiations Boaz was planning would not only shape her future but Naomi's as well. So she told Naomi everything she and Boaz had said and done. While she was talking, she opened the folds of her cape and poured the barley into a basket. "And Boaz was also concerned about you," she said. "He gave me all this grain so I wouldn't come home to you empty-handed."

Naomi looked to heaven with joy. God had answered her prayers. Ruth had found a husband and a home. A gracious and loving God would provide for them both. "Ruth," she said, "I'm confident Boaz will work everything out today. So let us be patient and wait until we see how things will turn out."

Betrothal and Marriage

In biblical times parents arranged marriages. Once a prospective wife had been chosen, a friend of the bride-groom would enter into negotiations with a representative of the future bride's father. In the ancient Jewish culture, women were seen as something of a liability. A daughter could not do the heavy field work that sons were able to do. As the subject of marriage was broached, the groom or his family were expected to compensate the future bride's family for the fact that she was a woman. Furthermore, it was customary for the bride's father to give his daughter a dowry (usually a sum of money that had been accumulating since her birth). He could use the interest from the dowry, but the dowry itself had to be kept in a trust in case she was ever widowed or divorced.

Once all arrangements had been made, the couple was "bound by vows," or betrothed to be married. Such vows were often brief statements carefully prepared by the groom to declare to all within hearing that the bride and groom from this day forward should be considered by all to be united in marriage. It was not unusual for both the bride's family and the groom's family to also make state-ments of commitment at this time, since marriage was also seen as a useful tool for forging new family alliances or business partnerships.

The betrothal lasted a year. Preparations for marriage were made. The man sought housing. Sometimes, in public places, the woman covered her face with a veil during this entire year.

The agreement could be broken only by a legal transaction similar in nature to a divorce in contemporary law. This transaction could only occur if the grounds for termination was adultery. (A betrothed or married woman found guilty of adultery could also be stoned to death.)

On her wedding day, the bride was adorned like a queen. She wore special wedding clothes lovingly made by her family. Her hair was braided with as many precious stones as her family could afford or borrow. The girls who dressed her also accompanied her throughout the day as her "companions."

The bridegroom also dressed in fine clothes and jewelry and was accompanied by "the friend of the groom." At the weddings of wealthy families, even guests had specially prepared wedding clothes provided for them.

At the end of the wedding day, the bridegroom walked with friends from his house to his bride's home. An honor guard followed as though he were a conquering hero. The bride veiled her face as she and her companions waited for them. Then the wedding couple and their companions walked back to the bridegroom's house, guests singing, dancing, and holding oil lamps to light the way. At some point the bride's veil was taken off and laid on the groom's shoulder. A declaration was made: "The government shall be upon his shoulder." Arriving at the groom's house, the bride and groom sat under a special canopy and the feast began.

The feast could last as long as seven days with much drinking, eating, dancing, and singing. Guests often would return home to carry out their day's work and then return to the celebration for the evening hours. Wedding feasts were important events in a community because they often provided opportunity for making new acquaintances, renewing old friendships, and arranging business transactions.

When Boaz got back to Bethlehem, he entered the town gate and stepped up onto the platform that was used for public meetings and for transacting business agreements. There he sat down on a bench and watched the first rays of dawn penetrate the early morning shadows. The warming rays of the sun brought life and vitality to the marketplace that spread out before him. A farmer's wife and her children lifted sacks of grain off their cart and set them out for sale; a herdsman staked two young goats under his canopy; and field workers began to trickle through the town gate. The workday was beginning.

Before long, the close relative Boaz had told Ruth about came walking by. "Good morning, my friend," said Boaz. "Please come over here and sit down."

The man sat down to see what Boaz had to say. Before explaining the situation to him, Boaz watched for town leaders to come by. He caught the attention of ten of them, asking them to witness the discussion he was about to initiate. He wanted them to support any agreement that might be reached. He knew that, by law, a transaction would be binding if it was upheld by at least two witnesses.

The town leaders agreed and sat down to hear the case. Then Boaz turned to his relative and began to explain the matter of Elimelech's property. He said, "Naomi, who has come back from Moab, is selling the fields that belonged to her late husband, Elimelech—our relative. I thought it was only right that I should inform you of Naomi's intentions. And I would also suggest, in the presence of these witnesses, that you consider buying Naomi's property. Since you are Elimelech's closest relative, you have the legal right to buy it. But, if you don't want to purchase the land, I need to know because, as the next closest relative, I'm willing to purchase it."

News traveled fast in little Bethlehem. The man had already heard all about Naomi's situation. He knew she was too old and frail to work the land herself. He realized that she would therefore be forced to sell it—probably as soon as the harvest was over. As Elimelech's closest relative, he knew that if anyone else bought the land from Naomi, he had the right to buy it back—to keep it in the family. Since Boaz was forcing the issue, the man decided he might as well buy it now. It would be a good investment. So he answered, "I'm willing to buy the property."

Boaz had foreseen this response. This man was also shrewd in business, so Boaz added, "You should know, how-ever, that on the day you buy the land, I intend to marry Ruth. And you know that if God should bless us with a son, he could immediately claim rights to the family's land in Mahlon's name." (Mahlon was the name of Ruth's deceased husband, one of Elimelech and Naomi's two sons.) Although he was under no obligation to do so, Boaz had earlier agreed to marry Ruth. He was now declaring his willingness to protect Naomi, her property, and Mahlon's name as well.

Hearing this, the man realized that buying Naomi's property might be a bad investment. If a son was born to Ruth and Boaz in Mahlon's name, not only could that son claim the

The Kinsman-Redeemer Laws

According to Deuteronomy 25:5-9, if a man died without leaving a male heir, his brother was to marry the widow. The widow herself could, in fact, legally claim the right to marry her brother-in-law. The first son born to this marriage was to bear the name of the deceased brother, in order to preserve any inheritance that remained intact.

This law, however, did not apply in the story of Ruth. Boaz was not a brother-in-law to either Naomi or Ruth. It may have been the custom in Bethlehem to apply this law to the nearest relative. Ruth could therefore lay claim to a marriage with Boaz because she was the widow of Mahlon, a close relative of Boaz.

Naomi knew there was a closer relative than Boaz, but she was confident that he would yield his rights to Boaz. Numbers 27:8-11 and Leviticus 25:25 discuss those laws concerning inheriting and redeeming the property of a man who dies without a son. His property went first to his daughter. If there was no daughter, the property then went to his brothers. If there were no brothers, the property went to his nearest relative.

If the heir's financial status forced him or her to sell the property, the nearest relative was expected to buy it back, or redeem it. If there was no relative to buy it back, the heir could redeem it later when his or her financial situation improved.

Ruth could claim the right to be married to the next of kin. The next of kin was expected to carry out his duty to marry the childless widow. If he did not carry out his duty, he forfeited the privilege of buying back the property. In Bethlehem at the time when Ruth lived there, it must have been the custom that if the nearest relative refused both to marry the widow and redeem the property, the next nearest relative could do so.

Binding Agreements

The public life of an Israelite village was concentrated near its main gate. The marketplace was located there, and it was there that matters of law were brought before the elders of the community. The elders also served as the official witnesses of transactions such as the one in which Boaz agreed to marry Ruth. In this case, it was Boaz' hope that Ruth's deceased husband's nearest kinsman would give up all rights and claims to her family's property. A man renouncing his property rights would remove a sandal and present it to the new property holder. Everyone under-stood the significance of this gesture. In the same way that signatures finalize legal transactions today, it was the final step in consummating the agreement. If witnessed by ten elders and corroborated by no fewer than two of them under challenge, the agreement was considered legally binding.

family land but Naomi wouldn't even be legally obligated to return the money he would have paid for her property. So he said: "Then I can't buy the land. I could jeopardize my own inheritance by taking such a risk. Boaz, I give you the right to buy the property for yourself."

The man had made up his mind. His decision was final. He would give up his right to purchase Naomi's property. To legalize the agreement, he took off his sandal and gave it to Boaz in full view of the ten witnesses. This symbolized that he had given up the right to "walk on the land," to possess it. The town leaders who witnessed this action would now confirm that the deal had been finalized and was legally binding.

Then Boaz summarized the contract that he and his relative had agreed upon. He announced to the leaders and the other people who had gathered to listen to the proceedings: "Today you are all witnesses that I have purchased from Naomi all the property that belonged to Elimelech and his sons, Kilion and Mahlon. I have also acquired the right to take Mahlon's widow, Ruth, as my wife so the inheritance can remain in her deceased husband's name. In this way Mahlon's name will live on in his family and in the public records. Today you are witnesses to these transactions."

Then the people responded: "We are happy to be witnesses to your kindness. May the Lord bless your wife, Ruth, with children, just as he blessed Rachel and Leah, the wives of our ancestor Jacob. May you prosper, and may your name always be as honored in Bethlehem as it is today. May the children born to you and your wife be as honorable as your ancestor Perez, the son of Judah and Tamar."

So Boaz married Ruth as he had promised. They lived together as man and wife. And, to everyone's delight, Ruth became pregnant. Before the next barley harvest, she gave birth to a healthy baby boy.

The women of the village paused from their daily chores and smiled as Naomi entered the marketplace, sat down on a bench, and placed the basket she was carrying beside her. In it was her infant grandson. What a difference a year can make! A year ago, these women had been buzzing about how bitter and destitute Naomi had become as she returned to Bethlehem, accompanied by a Moabite stranger. Today they would rejoice with Naomi over her good fortune and the blessings Ruth had brought into her life. "Praise the Lord!" they said to Naomi. "Today the Lord has given you someone to take care of you. May your grandson's name become famous throughout Israel. May he restore your life and support you in your old age. What a blessing Ruth's love has been! Her love for you has been worth more than having seven sons." Everyone knew Naomi would fill a special role in the life of Ruth's child—caring for him like a mother.

A baby's cry penetrated the clamor of the busy market-place. Naomi gazed at the child who had been sleeping in the cushioned basket at her side. She gently picked him up and laid him on her lap, smiling into his sparkling eyes. She felt like he was her own flesh and blood.

The women of the town gathered around Naomi to admire the precious infant. Confident that the child would inherit the best qualities of Ruth and Boaz, the women named him Obed, which means "the one who serves."

Again God had carried out his plan. Ruth was now a woman of high standing in Bethlehem. Her steadfast love had sustained a once-bitter Naomi through her darkest hours. Because of Boaz' actions at the town gate, Obed was now legally Naomi's grandson and heir to her property. Her life was full again.

But God's plans were more far-reaching than even Ruth or Naomi or Boaz could have imagined. For Obed would grow up and marry. His wife would bless him with a son named Jesse. And Jesse too would grow up and have a family. The youngest of Jesse's sons would be a shepherd boy named David—the same David who became the king of Israel. And centuries later another descendant of this family would be born in Bethlehem, "the house of bread." The child's name would be Jesus, the long-awaited Messiah, our Savior, the Shepherd-King of God's people, the Bread of Life eternal. In him God's plans would be fulfilled for all people of all times.

The Ancestry of Our Savior

The list of ten names noted in Ruth 4:18-22 was never meant to be a complete genealogy. In fact, the ten generations listed here span more than seven centuries. Instead, the purpose of this list is to emphasize a kind of metaphorical truth already in place with Adam and Eve in the Garden of Eden. This truth is that from the seed of a woman, God had promised to send a Redeemer to buy us back from the curse of sin. Just as sin has been passed down from parents to children, so also have God's promises been physically passed down in a linear manner through one family that can, at least in theory, be traced back to the very beginning of the human race.

Perez through David

Perez was the father of Hezron,
Hezron the father of Ram,
Ram the father of Amminadab,
Amminadab the father of Nahshon,
Nahshon the father of Salmon,
Salmon the father of Boaz,
Boaz the father of Obed,
Obed the father of Jesse,
and Jesse the father of David.

When you and I plan things, our plans are never implemented as exactly and precisely as we have planned. Sometimes we do not have enough of the facts in anticipation of our plans. Other times our gifts prove to be imperfect; a lacking here or there will alter the outcome. Things change—sometimes without warning. People change. Circumstances change. We change. Events spin out of our control.

From before the beginning of time, God has planned many things. He knows all the facts in advance. He has perfect foresight and insight. He is powerful and just and loving. And he does not change. The outcome of his plans is never altered. And the outcome is always for the good of his people.

Ruth, Boaz, Naomi, and the other believers of their time did not know how God would carry out his plan of salvation. They did not know when it would occur or where. But in their hearts of simple, childlike faith, they believed that whatever the outcome, it would happen according to his holy will. And they trusted that his will was always aimed at serving the welfare of his dear people.

You and I have the benefit of knowing the rest of Ruth's story. With the rearview mirror of hindsight and the inspired words of Scripture to tell us, we know that in this story, God's good and gracious purpose was accomplished. Through faithful Ruth and the generosity of a kind Boaz, God kept the hope of a Savior from sin alive for many more generations. This is yet another example testifying to the sureness of God's covenant; he has never forgotten his people or his promise.

Centuries later, from the ancestral line of Ruth and Boaz,

EPILOG

came Jesus, the King of heaven born in a humble Bethlehem stable—the long-awaited liberator from sin and its eternal curse—the fulfillment of God's promise. How great is our God, and how worthy of our praise! For he has brought all things to pass, including his eternal plan for our salvation.